Self-Inspection Handbook

for NISP Contractors

I0411548

Center for Development of Security Excellence

CD:SE

Learn. Perform. Protect.

November 2013

Self-Inspection Handbook for NISP Contractors
TABLE OF CONTENTS

ELEMENTS OF INSPECTION

INSPECTION ADDENDUM

SELF-INSPECTION HANDBOOK FOR NISP CONTRACTORS

The Contractor Security Review Requirement

> "Contractors shall review their security system on a continuing basis and shall also conduct a formal self-inspection at intervals consistent with risk management principles." **[1-206b, NISPOM]**

The Self-Inspection Handbook for NISP Contractors

The National Industrial Security Program Operating Manual (NISPOM) requires all participants in the National Industrial Security Program (NISP) to conduct their own security reviews (self-inspections). This Self-Inspection Handbook is designed as a job aid to assist you in complying with this requirement. It is not intended to be used as a checklist only. Rather it is intended to assist you in developing a viable self-inspection program specifically tailored to the classified needs of your cleared company. You will also find we have included various techniques that will help enhance the overall quality of your self-inspection.

The Elements of Inspection

The Self-Inspection Checklist contained within this handbook addresses basic NISPOM requirements through a series of questions arranged according to "Elements of Inspection." It is important to know that not all "Elements of Inspection" will apply to every cleared company. Before beginning your self-inspection, it is recommended that you review the "Elements of Inspection" to determine which ones are applicable to your facility's involvement in the NISP. Then use those elements to customize a self-inspection checklist unique to your security program.

There are five "Elements of Inspection" that are common to ALL cleared companies participating in the NISP and should be incorporated into your customized self-inspection check list: (A) Facility Security Clearance (FCL), (B) Access Authorizations, (C) Security Education, (D) FOCI, and (E) Classification. Any remaining elements need to only be covered if they relate to your security program. If you have questions about the relevancy of any element of inspection for your facility, please contact your Industrial Security Representative (IS Rep) for guidance. A look at your Standard Practice Procedure (SPP), if you have one, may also provide clues. Of course, as your program becomes more involved with classified information (e.g., changing from a non-possessing to a possessing facility), you will have to expand your self-inspection checklist to include those additional elements of inspection.

Also remember that not all of the questions (requirements) within each element may relate to your program. Since each question includes a NISPOM paragraph citation, review each requirement against the context of your industrial security program. If your involvement with classified information invokes the requirement, your procedures should comply with it and your self-inspection should assess your compliance. Reading all questions in the relevant elements of inspection will help you become more knowledgeable of the NISPOM requirements. In all cases, the regulatory guidance takes priority over company established procedures.

Self-Inspection Process

To be most effective it is suggested that you look at your self-inspection as a three-step process: 1) pre-inspection, 2) self-inspection, and 3) post-inspection.

1) PRE-INSPECTION.

So that you are fully prepared for your self-inspection, you want to start by conducting your pre-inspection research: 1) identify all security elements that apply, 2) familiarize yourself with how your company's business is structured and organized (it may have an impact on your company's security procedures), 3) identify who you will need to talk to and what records you may want to review, 4) prepare a list of questions and topics that need to be covered, (5) know your facility's physical layout (i.e., where the classified material is stored, worked on, etc.), and (6) have knowledge of the processes involved in the classified programs at your facility.

Remember, your primary sources of information during your self-inspection are your *documents* and *people.* Take the time to adequately prepare yourself by reviewing documentation you already have on-hand. This includes: the results of your last DSS security vulnerability assessment, your current DD Form 254s and classification guides, any recent company press releases or publications, your company web-site, any security records you may have on hand, and the JPAS records for your cleared employees.

Once you have completed your pre-inspection research, your next step is to set the date to conduct your self-inspection. Once your date is established, meet with your senior management team so they can understand the importance of your self-inspection and provide the support you need to be effective. Also take the time to meet with program and department managers to let them know what support you might need from them during the self-inspection process. Finally, make a formal announcement so that your employees will know what to expect.

The last thing you want to do before moving onto the actual self-inspection is to choose your Inspection Strategy. There are three basic methods for conducting your self-inspection: Programmatic, Comprehensive, and Combination. At the end of this handbook we give you an example of the Programmatic method. For more information regarding these inspection methods, please consider taking our NISP Self-Inspection Course (http://www.cdse.edu/catalog/elearning/IS130.html).

2) SELF-INSPECTION.

The self-inspection process includes gathering information about each of the inspection elements that apply to your company's classified involvement. Your job as the FSO is to *verify* and *validate* that your facility security program is in compliance with applicable NISPOM requirements and that all classified information entrusted to your company is adequately protected. To do this, simply review the self-inspection questions against the appropriate documentation (including your classified information) and the people (including their actions) involved in the facility's industrial security program. This is where the self-inspection checklist comes in handy. It not only provides you with the NISPOM requirements, but organizes them into elements of common security concern. These elements should not be viewed independently during your self-inspection, but interdependently, as it will become obvious to you that they frequently interrelate.

During the self-inspection, you want to ensure that you take the time to explain the self-inspection process and what is to be expected to each employee you interview. This may be their first time going through any type of inspection; people tend to be reluctant to provide information when they don't know why they are providing it. Don't limit yourself to just talking with your employees. Look at their processes, have them demonstrate what they do when working with classified information, spot check documentation, and inspect security equipment to include any Intrusion Detection Systems (IDS), Information Systems, and security containers that they have access to or are responsible for.

A quality self-inspection depends on your ability to ask questions and listen to the answers you receive. They may identify security problems you would otherwise not be brought to your attention. Seek information about *current* procedures and *change*s which could affect future actions. Get out of your office and into the working environment. Check security records, test security systems, and most importantly talk to people!

There are certain titled employees you may want to target for interviews during your self-inspection to include your key management personnel, both your cleared and uncleared employees, the webmaster, program managers, human resources personnel, contracts personnel, the receptionist, and mailroom personnel to name a few.

Here are some general interviewing techniques and questions to assist you in conducting quality interviews during your self-inspection:

General Interviewing Techniques

☐ All questions should be asked in the present and future sense.

☐ Talk in a conversational tone and maintain eye contact.

☐ Let people tell their story. Ask open ended questions (using who, what, where, when, why, and how).

☐ Avoid leading questions.

☐ Let people show you how they perform their jobs that involve compliance with a security program requirement.

☐ Follow-up the checklist questions with your own questions.

☐ Keep good notes for future reference and document corrective actions.

Suggested Questions When Interviewing Uncleared Employees:

☐ What is classified information?

☐ How would you know if something was classified?

☐ If you found unprotected, classified information, what would you do?

☐ Have you ever heard classified information being discussed?

☐ Have you ever come into possession of classified materials? How?

Suggested Questions When Interviewing Cleared Employees:

☐ What is your job title/responsibility?

☐ What is the level of your security clearance?

☐ Why are you cleared (describe the contract or programs that require you to be cleared)?

☐ How long have you been cleared?

☐ If recently cleared, what were the processes/steps in applying for your security clearance?

☐ When was your last access to classified information and at what level?

☐ Have you ever accessed classified information outside of this facility?

☐ What are the procedures for going on classified visits?

☐ How about visitors coming here for a classified visit?

☐ Did anyone else from the facility accompany you on this visit?

☐ What procedures did you follow prior to your classified visit?

☐ Did you take any classified notes or bring any classified information back to the facility?

☐ What procedures were followed to protect this information?

☐ Where is this information now?

☐ Have you ever allowed visitors to have access to classified information?

☐ How did you determine their need-to-know?

☐ Have you ever been approached by anyone requesting classified information?

☐ Do you ever work overtime and access classified information?

☐ When was the last time that you had a security briefing?

☐ What can you recall from this briefing?

☐ Can you recall any of the following being addressed in briefings?

Risk Management	Job Specific Security Brief
Public Release	Safeguarding Responsibilities
Adverse Information	Counterintelligence Awareness

☐ What is meant by the term *adverse information* and how would you report it?

☐ Can you recall any other reportable items?

☐ What is meant by the term *suspicious contact* and how would you report one?

☐ Have you ever been cited for a security violation, infraction, or incident?

☐ What would you do if you committed a security violation, infraction, or discovered one?

☐ Do you have the combination to any storage containers, access to any Closed Areas, etc.?

☐ What are the security requirements regarding combinations to security containers?

☐ Who, other than yourself, has access to these containers?

☐ How do you keep track or maintain your knowledge of the combination?

☐ Is a record maintained of the safe combination? If so, where?

☐ Do you generate or derivatively classify information? Tell me about it.

☐ What security controls are established?

☐ How do you know it's classified?

☐ Describe the training you received prior to derivatively classifying or generating classified.

☐ Where do you typically work on classified information?

☐ What procedures do you follow to protect classified information while working on it?

☐ What do you do with classified information?

☐ Do you ever use a computer to generate classified information?

☐ How do you mark this information?

☐ What information or references do you use when classifying information?

☐ Please produce the classification guidance that you used. Is it accurate?

☐ What would you do if you determined that the classification guidance was not accurate?

☐ What are the security procedures for publishing classified papers, etc.?

☐ Do you ever handcarry any classified information outside of your company?

☐ What procedures do you employ when handcarrying classified material?

☐ Have you ever reproduced classified information? Describe the procedures.

☐ Have you ever destroyed classified information? What procedures were used?

☐ Do you have any questions regarding security?

NOTE: In addition to asking questions, it is a good idea to ask cleared employees to demonstrate how they perform their security-related tasks, e.g., "Show me what you do before processing classified information on your computer" or "Show me how you prepare a package for shipment." This will allow you not only to verify what the correct procedures are, but to ensure those procedures are being carried out and that classified information is being protected.

3) POST- INSPECTION.

Once you have completed your self-inspection, you are not yet done. In fact, your real work has just begun. Make sure you take whatever action is necessary to correct any problem areas you identified during your self-inspection. You may even have to develop additional security education materials to address these problem areas.

It is important to provide immediate feedback to both your management and employees. After all, you spent a lot of time to get them vested in this process. Make sure to keep them vested by providing good, honest feedback. Remember the information you gathered during your self-inspection can only help to improve the overall effectiveness of your security program. Make sure to highlight any successes as well as any problem areas requiring corrective action found during your self-inspection. It is always a good idea to make an effort to provide "kudos" to any of your employees that were found to go above and beyond your established security procedures to ensure the protection of your classified material.

Finally, you might consider sharing your self-inspection results with your DSS IS Rep. Let them know how hard you worked to conduct a thorough self-inspection and the actions taken to maintain a successful security program. Your IS Rep is also a valuable resource should you encounter problem areas during your self-inspection and aren't quite sure how to resolve them.

SELF-INSPECTION CHECKLIST

As you work through the Self-Inspection Checklist, answer each question that applies to your security program. For those that do not apply, simply annotate N/A. We also recommend that for each question that applies to your security program, you utilize the space titled *Validation* to document the actions taken to validate the answer provided.

You will also notice that we have provided links to various resources available in our FSO Toolkit to assist you in verifying the effectiveness of your security program. Feel free to take a look at these resources to assist you in conducting the most thorough self-inspection possible.

You are now ready to conduct the best self-inspection ever – good luck!

A. FACILITY CLEARANCE

NISPOM REF:	Question:	YES	NO	N/A
1-302g(3)	Have all changes (e.g. changes in ownership, operating name or address, Key Management Personnel (KMP) information, previously reported FOCI information, or action to terminate business) affecting the condition of the FCL been reported to your DSS IS Rep? *VALIDATION:*	☐	☐	☐
2-100c	Has the company's FCL been used for advertising or promotional purpose? *VALIDATION:*	☐	☐	☐
2-104	Are the senior management official, the FSO, and other KMP cleared as required in connection with the FCL? *VALIDATION:*	☐	☐	☐
2-106a-b	Have the proper exclusion actions been conducted for uncleared company officials? *RESOURCE:* Temporary Exclusion Resolution for KMP Template under Key Management Personnel at: http://www.cdse.edu/toolkits/fsos/personnel-clearances.html *VALIDATION:*	☐	☐	☐
2-108 2-109	Are you familiar with the way your facility is organized and structured? *RESOURCE:* Business Structure Job Aid under Facility Clearance at: http://www.cdse.edu/toolkits/fsos/facility-clearance.html *VALIDATION:*	☐	☐	☐

A. FACILITY CLEARANCE				
NISPOM REF:	**Question:**	**YES**	**NO**	**N/A**
2-108	Does the home office have an FCL at the same or higher level than any cleared facility within the Multiple Facility Organization (MFO)? *RESOURCE:* ISL 2006-02 #7 Clearing Branch Offices Under Facility clearances at: http://www.cdse.edu/toolkits/fsos/facility-clearance.html *VALIDATION:*	☐	☐	☐
2-111	Are the DD Forms 441 and/or 441-1, SF 328, and Letter of Notification of Facility clearance (DSS FL 381-R), available, properly executed, and maintained in current status (verify that there have been no changes since your last DSS security vulnerability assessment)? *RESOURCE:* Copy of these forms are available under Forms at: http://www.cdse.edu/toolkits/fsos/facility-clearance.html *VALIDATION:*	☐	☐	☐

B. ACCESS AUTHORIZATIONS

NISPOM REF:	Question:	YES	NO	N/A
2-200b	Is all the information in Joint Personnel Adjudication System/Joint Clearance and Access Verification System (JPAS/JCAVS) pertaining to your cleared employees accurate and up to date? VALIDATION:	☐	☐	☐
	Does each employee's JPAS/JCAVS record indicate an appropriate "eligibility" and "access?" VALIDATION:	☐	☐	☐
	Have all JPAS/JCAVS users and account managers been officially appointed, issued unique usernames and passwords, and given the appropriate level in JPAS/JCAVS? VALIDATION:	☐	☐	☐
	Have all JPAS/JCAVS users received training appropriate for their duties and responsibilities? VALIDATION:	☐	☐	☐
2-200d	Are the numbers of clearances held to a minimum consistent with contractual requirements? VALIDATION:	☐	☐	☐
2-202a	Are employees in process for security clearances notified in writing that review of the SF 86 is for adequacy and completeness only and that the information will be used for no other purpose within the company? VALIDATION:	☐	☐	☐
2-202b	Are procedures in place to ensure that the applicant's SF 86 and fingerprint cards are authentic, legible, and complete to avoid clearance processing delays? VALIDATION:	☐	☐	☐

B. ACCESS AUTHORIZATIONS

NISPOM REF:	Question:	YES	NO	N/A
2-202b	Are original, signed copies of the SF 86 and releases retained until the applicant's eligibility for access to classified information has been granted or denied, and then destroyed? **RESOURCE:** Notice to contractors Regarding Retention of SF 86 under Forms at: http://www.cdse.edu/toolkits/fsos/personnel-clearances.html **VALIDATION:**	☐	☐	☐
2-205	Are all pre-employment offers based on acceptance to begin employment within 30 days of granting eligibility for a Personnel Clearance (PCL)? **RESOURCE:** ISL 2009-02, #2 Pre-employment Clearance Action under Industrial Security Letters at: http://www.cdse.edu/toolkits/fsos/personnel-clearances.html **VALIDATION:**	☐	☐	☐
2-207	Has citizenship been verified for each initial PCL applicant? **RESOURCE:** ISL 2011-02 Acceptable Proof of Citizenship under Industrial Security Letters at: http://www.cdse.edu/toolkits/fsos/personnel-clearances.html **VALIDATION:**	☐	☐	☐
1-302	Have reports on all cleared employees been submitted to the Personnel Security Management Office for Industry (PSMO-I) or the DSS IS Rep as required? NOTE: JPAS/JCAVS may be used for submission of some of these reports. **VALIDATION:**	☐	☐	☐

C. SECURITY EDUCATION

NISPOM REF:	Question:	YES	NO	N/A
3-102	Have you, as the FSO, completed security training considered appropriate by the Cognizant Security Agency (CSA)? **RESOURCES:** ISL 2012-03 FSO Training <u>and</u> FSO Curricula Brochure under Resources for FSOs at: http://www.cdse.edu/toolkits/fsos/security-education.html. *VALIDATION:*	☐	☐	☐
3-103, 9-202	Have you, as the FSO, received special security briefings and debriefings provided by DSS or Government Contracting Activity (GCA) when required? *VALIDATION:*	☐	☐	☐
3-104	Do cleared persons at other locations receive the required security training? How is this training provided? *VALIDATION:*	☐	☐	☐
3-105	Are SF 312s properly executed by cleared employees prior to accessing classified information and forwarded to PSMO-I for retention? **RESOURCE:** ISL 2006-02 SF 312 Date in JPAS under Industrial Security Letters at: http://www.cdse.edu/toolkits/fsos/personnel-clearances.html *VALIDATION:*	☐	☐	☐
1-302f 3-105	Are refusals to execute the SF 312 reported to PSMO-I? *VALIDATION:*	☐	☐	☐
3-106	Do initial security briefings contain all required information? *VALIDATION:*	☐	☐	☐

C. SECURITY EDUCATION

NISPOM REF:	Question:	YES	NO	N/A
3-107	Does the security education program include refresher security briefings? When was the last refresher training conducted? Were all employees provided this training? **VALIDATION:**	☐	☐	☐
1-205, 3-100, 3-108	Are all cleared employees provided with security training and briefings commensurate with their involvement with classified information? **VALIDATION:**	☐	☐	☐

Interview personnel throughout the work place to determine the effectiveness of your security education program. What do the employees remember from the last security briefing? Have them demonstrate the application of security procedures in the performance of their jobs.

3-108	Are cleared employees debriefed at the time of a PCL's termination, suspension, revocation, or upon termination of the FCL? **VALIDATION:**	☐	☐	☐
1-300	Are there established internal procedures that ensure cleared employees are aware of their responsibilities for reporting pertinent information to the FSO as required? **VALIDATION:**	☐	☐	☐
1-301, 1-302	Is there an effective procedure for submission of required reports to the FBI and to DSS? **VALIDATION:**	☐	☐	☐

C. SECURITY EDUCATION

NISPOM REF:	Question:	YES	NO	N/A
1-301	Do you have a process in place to report all Cyber Intrusions? **RESOURCE:** ISL 2013-05 Applicability of NISPOM Paragraph 1-301 Reporting Requirements to Cyber Intrusions under Industrial Security Letters at: http://www.cdse.edu/toolkits/fsos/reporting.html **VALIDATION:**	☐	☐	☐
1-302a	Have you reviewed and submitted all adverse information reports received since the last DSS security vulnerability assessment? **RESOURCES:** ISL 2011-04 Adverse Information and ISL 2006-02 Reporting Participation in Rehabilitation Programs as Adverse Information under Industrial Security Letters at: http://www.cdse.edu/toolkits/fsos/reporting.html **VALIDATION:**	☐	☐	☐
1-302b	Have you submitted all suspicious contact reports as required? **RESOURCES:** Webinar: What Information is Reportable as a Suspicious Contact Report and Suspicious Contact Report Template under Reporting at: http://www.cdse.edu/toolkits/fsos/reporting.html **VALIDATION:**	☐	☐	☐
1-303	Do your cleared employees, as well as yourself, know what a violation is and to whom you should report it? **RESOURCES:** Administrative Inquiry (AI) Job Aid for Industry job aid under Reporting and ISL 2006-02 Reports Submitted to the CSA under Industrial Security Letters at: http://www.cdse.edu/toolkits/fsos/reporting.html **VALIDATION:**	☐	☐	☐
1-304	Is there a graduated scale of administrative disciplinary action that is applied in the event of employee violations or negligence? **VALIDATION:**	☐	☐	☐

C. SECURITY EDUCATION				
NISPOM REF:	**Question:**	**YES**	**NO**	**N/A**
1-204 6-103	Do you cooperate with officially credentialed representatives of Federal Agencies conducting inspections, audits and investigations? **RESOUIRCE:** ISL 2010-01 Cooperation with Contractors That Are Officially Credentialed Representatives of Federal Agencies under Industrial Security Letters at: http://www.cdse.edu/toolkits/fsos/new-fso.html **VALIDATION:**	☐	☐	☐
1-207	Are employees aware of the various Defense Hotline numbers? **RESOURCE:** DoD Hotline Posters under Resources for FSOs at: http://www.cdse.edu/toolkits/fsos/security-education.html **VALIDATION:**	☐	☐	☐

D. CONSULTANTS				
NISPOM REF:	**Question:**	**YES**	**NO**	**N/A**
2-212	Have you and your consultants jointly executed a "consultant agreement" setting forth your respective security responsibilities? **RESOURCE:** Consultant Agreement under Forms at: http://www.cdse.edu/toolkits/fsos/personnel-clearances.html. **VALIDATION:**	☐	☐	☐
2-212	Does the consultant possess classified material at his/her place of business? **VALIDATION:**	☐	☐	☐

For security administrative purposes, the consultant shall be considered an employee of the using contractor.

E. STANDARD PRACTICE PROCEDURES (SPP)				
NISPOM REF:	Question:	YES	NO	N/A
1-202	Does your company have a Standard Practice Procedure (SPP)? Is this available to your cleared employees? **VALIDATION:**	☐	☐	☐
1-202	If your company has an SPP in place, is it current and does it adequately implement the requirements of the NISPOM? **VALIDATION:**	☐	☐	☐

Remember that a written SPP must be prepared when the FSO or the CSA believes it is necessary for the proper safeguarding of classified information. 1-202

F. SUBCONTRACTING

NISPOM REF:	Question:	YES	NO	N/A
7-101	Are all required actions completed prior to release or disclosure of classified information to sub-contractors? **RESOURCES:** Short: DD Form 254, Guide for the Preparation of a DD Form 254 and How to complete a DD Form 254 Performance Support Guide under Information about Working on Classified contracts at: http://www.cdse.edu/toolkits/fsos/new-fso.html **VALIDATION:**	☐	☐	☐
7-101b(1)	Are the clearance status and safeguarding capability of all subcontractors determined as required? **VALIDATION:**	☐	☐	☐
7-101b(2)	Do requests for facility clearance or safeguarding include the required information? **RESOURCES:** Webinar: New Facility Clearance Sponsorship for GCA and Prime Contractors; Facility Clearance Sponsorship Letter and New Facility Clearance Sponsorship Pamphlet under Sponsorship at: http://www.cdse.edu/toolkits/fsos/facility-clearance.html **VALIDATION:**	☐	☐	☐
7-102	If your company is a prime contractor, have you incorporated adequate security classification guidance into each classified subcontract? **VALIDATION:**	☐	☐	☐
7-102a	Are original *Contract Security Classification Specifications* (DD 254) included with each classified solicitation? **VALIDATION:**	☐	☐	☐

F. SUBCONTRACTING		YES	NO	N/A
NISPOM REF:	**Question:**	YES	NO	N/A
7-102b	Are revised *Contract Security Classification Specifications* (DD 254) issued as necessary? ***VALIDATION:***	☐	☐	☐
7-103	If your company is a prime contractor, have you obtained approval from the GCA for subcontractor retention of classified information associated with a completed contract? ***VALIDATION:***	☐	☐	☐

G. VISIT CONTROL

NISPOM REF:	Question:	YES	NO	N/A
6-101	Are classified visits held to the minimum? *VALIDATION:*	☐	☐	☐
6-101	Are procedures established to ensure positive identification of visitors prior to disclosure of classified information? *VALIDATION:*	☐	☐	☐
6-101	Are procedures established to ensure that visitors are only afforded access to classified information consistent with their visit? (need-to-know) *VALIDATION:*	☐	☐	☐
6-102	Is disclosure of classified information based on need to know (a contractual relationship) or an assessment that the receiving contractor has a bona fide need to access classified information? *VALIDATION:*	☐	☐	☐
6-104	Are visit authorization requests sent and received through JCAVS whenever possible? *RESOURCE:* ISL 2006-02 Visit Authorization for DoE and ISL 2006-01 Visitor Authorization under Industrial Security Letters at: http://www.cdse.edu/toolkits/fsos/classified-visits.html *VALIDATION:*	☐	☐	☐
6-104	Do visit authorization requests include the required information and are they updated to reflect changes in the status of that information? *VALIDATION:*	☐	☐	☐
6-105	Are long-term visitors governed by the security procedures of the host contractor? *VALIDATION:*	☐	☐	☐

H. CLASSIFIED MEETINGS (Sponsored by the Government)		YES	NO	N/A
NISPOM REF:	**Question:**			
6-201	Has the government agency sponsoring the meeting approved all security arrangements, announcements, attendees, and the meeting location? ***RESOURCES:*** Procedural Guide for Conducting Classified Meetings <u>and</u> Webinar: Classified Meeting Requirements under Classified Meetings at: http://www.cdse.edu/toolkits/fsos/classified-visits.html ***VALIDATION:***	☐	☐	☐
6-201a	Did your request for authorization include all required information? ***VALIDATION:***	☐	☐	☐
6-201c	Have all security arrangements been approved by the authorizing agency? ***RESOURCE:*** Checklist for Classified Meetings under Classified Meetings at: http://www.cdse.edu/toolkits/fsos/classified-visits.html ***VALIDATION:***	☐	☐	☐
6-201c (2)	Is attendance limited to persons appropriately cleared who have the need-to-know? ***VALIDATION:***	☐	☐	☐
6-201c (3) and 6-202	Is prior written authorization obtained, from the relevant GCA, before disclosure of classified information? ***VALIDATION:***	☐	☐	☐

H. CLASSIFIED MEETINGS (Sponsored by the Government)

NISPOM REF:	Question:	YES	NO	N/A
6-202b	Has a copy of the disclosure authorization been furnished to the Government Agency sponsoring the meeting? **VALIDATION:**	☐	☐	☐

Remember that classified presentations can be delivered orally and/or visually. Copies of classified presentations, slides, etc. shall not be distributed at the meeting, but rather safeguarded and transmitted commensurate with the level of classification.

NISPOM REF:	Question:	YES	NO	N/A
6-203	Are your employees properly screened for clearance and need-to-know prior to attending classified meetings? **VALIDATION:**	☐	☐	☐

Authority to disclose classified information at meetings, whether by industry or government, must be granted by the Government Agency or Activity having classification jurisdiction. [6-202]

I. CLASSIFICATION

NISPOM REF:	Question:	YES	NO	N/A
4-102d	Have employees received appropriate training before they were authorized to make derivative classification decisions for you company? **RESOURCE:** ISL 2013-06 Derivative Classification under Industrial Security Letters at: http://www.cdse.edu/toolkits/fsos/safeguarding.html **VALIDATION:**	☐	☐	☐
4-102d	Are all derivative classifiers identified on the documents on which they made derivative classification decisions? **VALIDATION:**	☐	☐	☐
4-103	Is all classification guidance adequate and is the *Contract Security Classification Specification* (DD254) provided as required? **VALIDATION:**	☐	☐	☐
4-208	Is all derivatively classified material appropriately marked? **VALIDATION:**	☐	☐	☐
4-103	Do you possess a *Contract Security Classification Specification* (DD 254) for every classified contract issued to your company? **VALIDATION:**	☐	☐	☐
4-103c	Upon completion of a classified contract, did proper disposal of the relevant classified information take place or is the classified material being retained for two years? **VALIDATION:**	☐	☐	☐

I. CLASSIFICATION		YES	NO	N/A
NISPOM REF:	**Question:**			
4-104	Is improper or inadequate classification guidance being challenged? *VALIDATION:*	☐	☐	☐
4-105	Is contractor-developed information such as unsolicited proposals or other information not supporting the performance of a classified contract appropriately classified, marked, and protected? *VALIDATION:*	☐	☐	☐
4-107	Are downgrading and declassification actions accomplished as required, and is action taken to update records when changing the classification markings? *VALIDATION:*	☐	☐	☐

J. EMPLOYEE IDENTIFICATION		YES	NO	N/A
NISPOM REF:	**Question:**	**YES**	**NO**	**N/A**
5-410b	Do personnel possess the required identification card or badge when employed as couriers, handcarriers, or escorts? *VALIDATION:*	☐	☐	☐
5-313a	Did the manufacturer of your automated access control devices provide written assurance that it meets NISPOM 5-313 standards? *VALIDATION:*	☐	☐	☐

Security procedures should maximize the use of personal recognition verification for access to classified material. Note that the NISPOM makes only passing reference to IDs and badges for use in specific instances. When such programs are employed as part of your security-in-depth procedures, the specifics should be reviewed with your IS Rep.

K. FOREIGN OWNERSHIP, CONTROL, OR INFLUENCE (FOCI)

NISPOM REF:	Question:	YES	NO	N/A
	The following questions apply to all contractors:			
2-302	Have there been changes in any of the information previously reported on your SF 328, *Certificate Pertaining to Foreign Interests*? ***RESOURCE:*** ISL 2009-03 What Constitutes a Reportable Materials Change under NISPOM 1-302g(5) or a Reportable Significant Change Under Paragraph 2-302 under Industrial Security Letters at: http://www.cdse.edu/toolkits/fsos/reporting.html ***VALIDATION:***	☐	☐	☐
2-302a	Has the presence of any/all FOCI factors been reported to your IS Rep in the manner prescribed? ***VALIDATION:***	☐	☐	☐
2-302b	Has the most current information pertaining to the SF 328 been provided to your DSS IS Rep? ***VALIDATION:***	☐	☐	☐
2-302b	Has your DSS IS Rep been notified of negotiations for merger, acquisition, or takeover by a foreign interest? ***VALIDATION:***	☐	☐	☐

The SF 328 Completion Instructions should be used to ensure your SF 328 contains current and accurate information.

Visit the Facility Clearance Page of CDSEs FSO Toolkit - http://www.cdse.edu/toolkits/fsos/facility-clearance.html - to access an electronic copy of the SF 328 with instructions, FOCI Mitigation Instruments, and a Technology Control Plan.

K. FOREIGN OWNERSHIP, CONTROL, OR INFLUENCE (FOCI)				
NISPOM REF:	Question:	YES	NO	N/A
	The following questions apply to facilities involved with FOCI:			
2-302b	Has a FOCI Mitigation Plan been submitted to your DSS IS Rep if necessary? *VALIDATION:*	☐	☐	☐
2-303c - (2a)	If cleared under a Special Security Agreement, has your company received a National Interest Determination (NID) for access to "proscribed information??" *Proscribed information is TOP SECRET/Restricted Data/Communications Security/Special Access Programs and Sensitive Compartmented Information. The special authorization must be manifested by a favorable national interest determination that must be program/project/contract specific from the appropriate GCA.* *VALIDATION:*	☐	☐	☐
2-306	Has a Government Security Committee been appointed from the Board of Directors under a Voting Trust, Proxy Agreement, Special Security Agreement (SSA), or Security Control Agreement (SCA)? *VALIDATION:*	☐	☐	☐
2-307	Have you developed a Technology Control Plan (TCP), approved by the DSS, when cleared under a Voting Trust, Proxy Agreement, SSA, or SCA? *VALIDATION:*	☐	☐	☐
2-308a	If operating under a Voting Trust, Proxy Agreement, or SCA, do your senior management officials meet annually with the DSS to review the effectiveness of the arrangement? *VALIDATION:*	☐	☐	☐
2-308b	Is an annual Implementation and Compliance Report submitted to your DSS IS Rep? *VALIDATION:*	☐	☐	☐

L. PUBLIC RELEASE				
NISPOM REF:	**Question:**	**YES**	**NO**	**N/A**
5-511	Was approval of the Government Contracting Activity obtained prior to public disclosure of information pertaining to a classified contract? *VALIDATION:*	☐	☐	☐
5-511a	Is a copy of each approved "request for release" retained for one assessment cycle for review by your DSS IS Rep? *VALIDATION:*	☐	☐	☐

M. CLASSIFIED STORAGE

NISPOM REF:	Question:	YES	NO	N/A
5-101	Do your cleared employees know where they can and can't hold classified discussions? *VALIDATION:*	☐	☐	☐
5-102a	Is there a system of security checks at the close of each working day to ensure that classified material is secured? Are these checks being accomplished in accordance with your established security procedures? *VALIDATION:*	☐	☐	☐
5-103	Is a system of perimeter controls maintained to deter or detect unauthorized introduction or removal of classified information from the facility? If so, when, where, and how are these being implemented? *VALIDATION:*	☐	☐	☐
5-103	Are signs posted at all entries and exits warning that anyone entering or departing is subject to an inspection of their personal effects? *VALIDATION:*	☐	☐	☐
5-104	Are procedures developed for the safeguarding of classified material during an emergency? *VALIDATION:*	☐	☐	☐
5-302	Is TOP SECRET classified information stored only in GSA-approved security containers, approved vaults, or approved Closed Areas with supplemental controls? *VALIDATION:*	☐	☐	☐

M. CLASSIFIED STORAGE		YES	NO	N/A
NISPOM REF:	**Question:**			
5-303, 307	Is all SECRET and Confidential material being stored in GSA-approved security containers, approved vaults, or closed areas? *RESOURCES:* ISL 2012-04 GSA Storage Equipment <u>and</u> SECRET Storage under Industrial Security Letters at: http://www.cdse.edu/toolkits/fsos/safeguarding.html. *VALIDATION:*	☐	☐	☐
5-306	Are Closed Areas constructed in accordance with the requirements of the NISPOM? *RESOURCE:* ISL 2006-02 Structural Integrity of Closed Areas under Industrial Security Letters at: http://www.cdse.edu/toolkits/fsos/safeguarding.html *VALIDATION:*	☐	☐	☐
5-306b	Has DSS approval been granted for the open shelf or bin storage commonly known as "open storage" of documents in Closed Areas? *RESOURCE:* ISL 2012-04 Open Shelf or Bin Storage under Industrial Security Letters at: http://www.cdse.edu/toolkits/fsos/safeguarding.html *VALIDATION:*	☐	☐	☐
5-308	Is the number of people possessing knowledge of the combinations to security containers kept to a minimum? *VALIDATION:*	☐	☐	☐
5-308a	Is a record of the names of people having knowledge of the combinations to security containers maintained? *VALIDATION:*	☐	☐	☐

M. CLASSIFIED STORAGE

NISPOM REF:	Question:	YES	NO	N/A
5-308b	Are security containers, vaults, cabinets, and other authorized storage containers kept locked when not under direct supervision of an authorized person? *VALIDATION:*	☐	☐	☐
5-308c-d	When combinations to classified containers are placed in written form, are they marked and stored as required? *VALIDATION:*	☐	☐	☐
5-309	Are combinations to security containers changed by authorized persons when required? *RESOURCE:* ISL 2006-02 Changing Combinations under Industrial Security Letters at: http://www.cdse.edu/toolkits/fsos/safeguarding.html *VALIDATION:*	☐	☐	☐
5-311a	If any of your approved security containers have been repaired, do you have a signed and dated certification provided by the repairer setting forth the method of repair that was used? *RESOURCE:* ISL 2006-01 Container Repairs under Industrial Security Letters at: http://www.cdse.edu/toolkits/fsos/safeguarding.html *VALIDATION:*	☐	☐	☐
5-313a	Do ID cards or badges used in conjunction with Automated Access Control Systems meet NISPOM standards? *VALIDATION:*	☐	☐	☐

The CSA may grant self-approval authority for closed area approvals provided the FSO meets specified qualification criteria. [5-306d]

N. CONTROLLED ACCESS AREAS

NISPOM REF:	Question:	YES	NO	N/A
5-303	Are supplemental controls in place for storage of SECRET material in Closed Areas? *VALIDATION:*	☐	☐	☐
5-305	Do Restricted Areas have clearly defined perimeters and is all classified material properly secured when the area is unattended? *VALIDATION:*	☐	☐	☐
5-306	Are persons without the proper clearance and need-to-know escorted at all times when in a Closed Area? *VALIDATION:*	☐	☐	☐

GSA approved security containers and approved vaults secured with locking mechanisms meeting Fed. Spec. FF-L-2740 and located in areas determined by the CSA to have security-in-depth do not require supplemental protection, NISPOM 5-307c.

See definition of Working Hours in NISPOM Appendix C.

NISPOM REF:	Question:	YES	NO	N/A
5-306	Are Closed Areas afforded supplemental protection during non-working hours? *VALIDATION:*	☐	☐	☐
5-312	If Supplanting Access Control Systems are used, do they meet NISPOM criteria, 5-313 & 5-314, and were they approved by the FSO prior to installation? *VALIDATION:*	☐	☐	☐

Watch entrances to Closed Areas to determine the procedures followed when supplanting access control devices are utilized. Are authorized users allowing unauthorized persons to piggy-back into the area?

N. CONTROLLED ACCESS AREAS

NISPOM REF:	Question:	YES	NO	N/A
5-900 5-901	Is your IDS approved by DSS prior to installation as supplemental protection and does it meet NISPOM or UL 2050 standards as required? *VALIDATION:*	☐	☐	☐
5-307 5-900	Does your IDS, utilized as supplemental protection, meet NISPOM requirements? *VALIDATION:*	☐	☐	☐

When guards are authorized as supplemental protection [5-307b], required patrol is two hours for TOP SECRET and four hours for SECRET.

5-902b	Are trained alarm monitors cleared to the SECRET level in continuous attendance when the IDS is in operation? *VALIDATION:*	☐	☐	☐
5-902d	Are alarms activated at the close of business? *VALIDATION:*	☐	☐	☐
5-902d-e	Are alarm records maintained as required? *VALIDATION:*	☐	☐	☐
5-903a (3)	Does the Central Alarm Station report failure to respond to alarm incidents to the CSA as required? *VALIDATION:*	☐	☐	☐

N. CONTROLLED ACCESS AREAS

NISPOM REF:	Question:	YES	NO	N/A
5-904 **5-905**	Are all IDS at the contractor facility installed by UL-listed installers and so certified? *VALIDATION:*	☐	☐	☐
5-904, 905	Has a UL 2050 CRZH certificate been issued? *VALIDATION:*	☐	☐	☐

Commercial Central Station Alarm Company guards do not require PCLs unless their duties afford them the opportunity to access classified material when responding to those alarms. [5-903a(2)]

O. MARKINGS				
NISPOM REF:	**Question:**	**YES**	**NO**	**N/A**
4-200 4-201	Is all classified material, regardless of its physical form, marked properly? *VALIDATION:*	☐	☐	☐
4-202, 4-203	Is all classified material conspicuously marked to show the name and address of the contractor responsible for its preparation, the identity (by name and position or personal identifier) of the classifier, the source(s) for derivative classification the date of preparation, and overall security markings? *VALIDATION:*	☐	☐	☐
4-206	Are all portions of documents containing classified information marked to show the highest level of classification, or that the portion is unclassified? *VALIDATION:*	☐	☐	☐
4-207	Are subject and title markings placed immediately before the item? *VALIDATION:*	☐	☐	☐
4-202, 4-208	Are all additional markings applied to classified information as required? *VALIDATION:*	☐	☐	☐
4-210	Are special types of classified material marked as required? *VALIDATION:*	☐	☐	☐

O. MARKINGS		YES	NO	N/A
NISPOM REF:	**Question:**	**YES**	**NO**	**N/A**
4-213	Are appropriate classification markings applied when the compilation of unclassified information requires protection? *VALIDATION:*	☐	☐	☐
4-217	Are downgrading/declassification notations properly completed? *VALIDATION:*	☐	☐	☐

Contractors must seek guidance from the GCA prior to taking any declassification action on material marked for automatic declassification. If approved by the GCA, all old classification markings shall be cancelled and new markings substituted whenever practical. [4-217a]

5-203b 4-214	When classified working papers are generated are they dated when created, marked with the overall classification, annotated "Working Papers," and destroyed when no longer needed? *VALIDATION:*	☐	☐	☐

Note: All working papers become final documents when transmitted and must be marked appropriately.

P. TRANSMISSION		YES	NO	N/A
NISPOM REF:	**Question:**	**YES**	**NO**	**N/A**
5-202 5-401	Are procedures established for proper receipt and inspection of classified transmittals? *VALIDATION:*	☐	☐	☐
5-401	Is classified information properly prepared for transmission outside the facility? *RESOURCE*: Video: Packaging Classified Documents under Transmission and Transportation at: http://www.cdse.edu/toolkits/fsos/safeguarding.html *VALIDATION:*	☐	☐	☐
5-401	Are receipts included with classified transmissions when required? *VALIDATION:*	☐	☐	☐
5-401b	Is a suspense system established to track transmitted documents until the signed receipt is returned? *VALIDATION:*	☐	☐	☐
5-402 5-403 5-404	Are authorized methods used to transmit classified outside the facility? *VALIDATION:*	☐	☐	☐

P. TRANSMISSION				
NISPOM REF:	Question:	YES	NO	N/A
5-503	Is disclosure of classified information between a parent and its subsidiary accomplished in the same manner as disclosure between a prime contractor and a subcontractor? *RESOURCE:* ISL 2011-03 Disclosure of Classified Information Between Parent and Subsidiaries Within a Corporate Family under Industrial Security Letters at: http://www.cdse.edu/toolkits/fsos/safeguarding.html *VALIDATION:*	☐	☐	☐

Remember that transmission of TOP SECRET outside of the facility requires written authorization from the Government Contracting Authority. [5-402]

Additionally, TOP SECRET material may NEVER be transmitted through the U.S. Postal Service.

2-100	Is the facility clearance and safeguarding capability of the receiving facility determined prior to transmission of classified information? *VALIDATION:*	☐	☐	☐
5-408	Does the contractor use a qualified carrier, authorized by the Government, when shipping classified material? *VALIDATION:*	☐	☐	☐
5-408 5-409	Are classified shipments made only in accordance with the NISPOM or instructions from the contracting authority? *VALIDATION:*	☐	☐	☐
5-410	Are couriers, handcarriers, and escorts properly briefed? *VALIDATION:*	☐	☐	☐

P. TRANSMISSION		YES	NO	N/A
NISPOM REF:	**Question:**	**YES**	**NO**	**N/A**
5-410	Is handcarrying of classified material outside the facility properly authorized, inventoried, and safeguarded during transmission? *VALIDATION:*	☐	☐	☐
5-411	Is handcarrying aboard commercial aircraft accomplished in accordance with required procedures? *VALIDATION:*	☐	☐	☐
5-412 5-413	Are sufficient numbers of escorts assigned to classified shipments and are they briefed on their responsibilities? *RESOURCE:* ISL 2006-01 Escorts and Transfers of Freight Under Industrial Security Letters at: http://www.cdse.edu/toolkits/fsos/safeguarding.html *VALIDATION:*	☐	☐	☐

Change: The requirement for escorts applies only when an escort is necessary to ensure the protection of classified information during transport. [5-412]

For information concerning international transmission of classified, see International Operations. NISPOM 10, Sec. 4

Q. CLASSIFIED MATERIAL CONTROLS

NISPOM REF:	Question:	YES	NO	N/A
5-100	Do your cleared employees understand their safeguarding responsibilities? *VALIDATION:*	☐	☐	☐

Facility walk-throughs are a good way to determine employees' knowledge of in-use controls for safeguarding classified information. Interview and observe how classified information is handled in the work place.

NISPOM REF:	Question:	YES	NO	N/A
5-200	Is your Information Management System (IMS) capable of facilitating the <u>retrieval</u> and <u>disposition</u> of classified material as required? *RESOURCE:* ISL 2006-01 Information Management System under Industrial Security Letters at: http://www.cdse.edu/toolkits/fsos/safeguarding.html *VALIDATION:*	☐	☐	☐

Evaluation of your IMS may be accomplished by conducting employee interviews. Your interview results, classified contract administration, and the results of classified materials reviewed at your facility will indicate whether or not your IMS is consistent with the NISPOM requirements.

Remember, the NISPOM requires a formal accountability system for Top Secret material, and an Information Management System (IMS) for Secret and Confidential material. [5-201; 5-203]

NISPOM REF:	Question:	YES	NO	N/A
5-201a	Has TOP SECRET control officials been designated at facilities that possess TOP SECRET information? *VALIDATION:*	☐	☐	☐
5-201a	Are TOP SECRET accountability records maintained as required and is an annual inventory conducted? *VALIDATION:*	☐	☐	☐
5-202	Is all classified material received directly by authorized personnel? *RESOURCE:* ISL 2006-01 Receiving Classified Material under Industrial Security Letters at: http://www.cdse.edu/toolkits/fsos/safeguarding.html *VALIDATION:*	☐	☐	☐

Q. CLASSIFIED MATERIAL CONTROLS

NISPOM REF:	Question:	YES	NO	N/A
5-103	Does your system of perimeter controls deter or detect unauthorized introduction or removal of classified information from the facility? *VALIDATION:*	☐	☐	☐
1-300 1-303	Are your cleared employees aware of their responsibility to promptly report the loss, compromise, or suspected compromise of classified information? *VALIDATION:*	☐	☐	☐
5-104	Are procedures adequate to protect classified during emergencies? *VALIDATION:*	☐	☐	☐

Conduct a walk-through inspection during lunch breaks, after hours, or on late work shifts when classified is being accessed.

R. REPRODUCTION				
NISPOM REF:	Question:	YES	NO	N/A
	Does the equipment used for classified reproduction have any sort of memory capability? If yes, the equipment may require accreditation as an Information System (IS). *VALIDATION:*	☐	☐	☐
5-600	Is reproduction of classified material kept to a minimum? *VALIDATION:*	☐	☐	☐
5-600	Is the reproduction of classified information accomplished only by properly cleared, authorized, and knowledgeable employees? *VALIDATION:*	☐	☐	☐
5-601	For Top Secret material, is reproduction authorization obtained as required? *VALIDATION:*	☐	☐	☐
5-602	Are reproductions of classified material reviewed to ensure that the markings are proper and legible? *VALIDATION:*	☐	☐	☐
5-603	Is a record of reproduction maintained for TS material and is it retained as required? *VALIDATION:*	☐	☐	☐

Any review of classified reproduction should include concern for waste (copy overruns, etc.), any materials used in production which may retain classified information or images requiring destruction or safeguarding, and type of copier used. A copier that includes any sort of memory may have to be accredited as an Information System rather than a copier.

S. DISPOSITION				
NISPOM REF:	Question:	YES	NO	N/A
5-700b	Are procedures established to review classified holdings on a recurring basis for the purpose of maintaining classified inventories to the minimum required for classified operations? *VALIDATION:*	☐	☐	☐
5-701 5-703	Is the disposition of classified material accomplished in accordance with the required schedule? *VALIDATION:*	☐	☐	☐
5-701 5-702	Is retention authority requested as required? *VALIDATION:*	☐	☐	☐
5-704	Is classified material destroyed as soon as possible after it has served its purpose? *VALIDATION:*	☐	☐	☐
5-705	Is an effective method of destruction employed that meets NISPOM standards? *VALIDATION:*	☐	☐	☐
5-706	Is classified material destroyed by appropriately cleared authorized personnel who fully understand their responsibilities? (may include appropriately cleared subcontractor personnel) *VALIDATION:*	☐	☐	☐

The NISPOM requires two persons for the destruction of TOP SECRET and one person for the destruction of SECRET and CONFIDENTIAL.

S. DISPOSITION				
NISPOM REF:	Question:	YES	NO	N/A
5-707	Are proper records maintained for the destruction of TOP SECRET classified information and do those who sign have actual knowledge of the material's destruction? *VALIDATION:*	☐	☐	☐
5-708	Is classified waste properly safeguarded until its timely destruction? *VALIDATION:*	☐	☐	☐

T. INFORMATION SYSTEMS

System No.	Overall Review Finding:	Reviewed By:	Date:

Administrative

NISPOM REF:	Question:	YES	NO	N/A
8-202	Has written accreditation for the System Security Plan (SSP) been obtained from DSS IAW Industrial Security Letter (ISL) 2009-01 which can be viewed at the following link: (http://dssinside.dss.mil)ISOM/isl.aspx)? *VALIDATION:*	☐	☐	☐
8-202a	If no, was interim approval granted? Up to 180 Days ☐ 181 to 360 Days ☐			
8-202	Did the user begin processing classified information before interim approval or written accreditation? *VALIDATION:*	☐	☐	☐
8-202a	If interim approval was granted, has the specified time period expired? *VALIDATION:*	☐	☐	☐
8-202g	Has the Information System Security Manager (ISSM) been authorized self-certification authority? *VALIDATION:*	☐	☐	☐
8-202g	If yes, does the ISSM certify all IS under the Master SSP? *VALIDATION:*	☐	☐	☐
	If yes, does the ISSM provide notification to DSS? *VALIDATION:*	☐	☐	☐
8-202d	Does the IS require reaccreditation based on 3 year limit? *VALIDATION:*	☐	☐	☐
8-202e	Has accreditation been withdrawn? *VALIDATION:*	☐	☐	☐

T. INFORMATION SYSTEMS

NISPOM REF:	Question:	YES	NO	N/A
8-202f	Has accreditation been invalidated? **_VALIDATION:_**	☐	☐	☐
8-202e	If withdrawn or invalidated, has memory and media been sanitized? **_VALIDATION:_**	☐	☐	☐

	Responsibilities			
8-101b	Has management published and promulgated an IS Security Policy? **_VALIDATION:_**	☐	☐	☐
8-101b	Has an ISSM been appointed? **_VALIDATION:_**	☐	☐	☐
8-103	If yes, are the ISSM's duties and responsibilities identified and being carried out? **_VALIDATION:_**	☐	☐	☐
8-104	Has the ISSM designated one or more Information System Security Officer(s) (ISSO(s)? **_VALIDATION:_**	☐	☐	☐
8-104	If yes, are the ISSO(s) duties and responsibilities identified and being carried out? **_VALIDATION:_**	☐	☐	☐
8-307	Are the privileged users' duties and responsibilities identified and understood? **_VALIDATION:_**	☐	☐	☐
8-307	Are the general users' responsibilities identified and understood? **_VALIDATION:_**	☐	☐	☐

T. INFORMATION SYSTEMS				
NISPOM REF:	**Question:**	**YES**	**NO**	**N/A**
	System Security Plan (SSP)			
8-402	What protection level (PL) is authorized? PL 1 ☐ PL 2 ☐ PL 3 ☐ PL 4 ☐ *VALIDATION:*			
8-401	What is the highest level of data processed? Confidential ☐ Secret ☐ Top Secret ☐ *VALIDATION:*			
	User Requirements			
Table 4	What is the clearance level of privileged users? Confidential ☐ Secret ☐ Top Secret ☐ *VALIDATION:*			
Table 4	What is the clearance level of general users? Confidential ☐ Secret ☐ Top Secret ☐ *VALIDATION:*			
Table 4	Do the users understand the need-to-know requirements of the authorized PL? *VALIDATION:*	☐	☐	☐
8-303a	How is the user granted access to the IS? User-IDs ☐ Personal identification ☐ Biometrics ☐ *VALIDATION:*			
	If passwords are used, does the user understand his/her responsibility for password creation deletion, changing, and length? *VALIDATION:*	☐	☐	☐

T. INFORMATION SYSTEMS

NISPOM REF:	Question:	YES	NO	N/A
8-311	Is the "user" involved in configuration management (i.e., adding/changing hardware, software, etc.)? *VALIDATION:*	☐	☐	☐
8-311	If yes, does the user understand and following the configuration management plan? *VALIDATION:*	☐	☐	☐
	IS Hardware			
8-311a	Does the SSP reflect the current hardware configuration? *VALIDATION:*	☐	☐	☐
8-311d	If not, do the maintenance logs reflect changes in the hardware configuration? *VALIDATION:*	☐	☐	☐
8-306a	Does the IS equipment bear appropriate classification markings? *VALIDATION:*	☐	☐	☐
	Physical Security			
8-308	How is the IS physically protected? (Check all that apply) Closed Area ☐ IS Defined Perimeter Boundary Area (Restricted Area) ☐ Approved Containers ☐ PDS [1] ☐ Approved Locks ☐ Access Control Devices ☐ Alarms ☐ Guards ☐ Patrols ☐ Seals ☐ Other (Specify) ☐ [1] Protected Distribution System ☐ Intrusion Detection System ☐ *VALIDATION:*			

T. INFORMATION SYSTEMS

NISPOM REF:	Question:	YES	NO	N/A
5-800	If closed area, are all construction requirements met? *VALIDATION:*	☐	☐	☐
5-306	Is access controlled by cleared employee, guard, or supplanting access control device? *VALIDATION:*	☐	☐	☐
5-306	If access is controlled by cleared employee, what criteria is used before granting access? *VALIDATION:*	☐	☐	☐
5-312	If access is controlled by a supplanting access control device, are all requirements met? *VALIDATION:*	☐	☐	☐
5-307	If required, is supplemental protection provided by guards or an approved IDS? *VALIDATION:*	☐	☐	☐
5-307b	If supplemental protection is provided by guards, are all requirements met? *VALIDATION:*	☐	☐	☐
5-900	If supplemental protection is provided by an IDS, are all requirements met? *VALIDATION:*	☐	☐	☐
5-306b	Is open shelf or bin storage of classified information, media, or equipment approved? *VALIDATION:*	☐	☐	☐
NSTISSI 7003	If classified wire lines leave the closed area, are all PDS construction requirements met? *VALIDATION:*	☐	☐	☐

T. INFORMATION SYSTEMS

NISPOM REF:	Question:	YES	NO	N/A
NSTISSI 7003	If PDS is used, are all inspection requirements followed? *VALIDATION:*	☐	☐	☐
NSTISSI 7003	If PDS is used, do they contain unclassified wire lines? *VALIDATION:*	☐	☐	☐
	If closed area has false ceilings or floors, are transmission lines not in a PDS inspected at least: Monthly (Security In-Depth) ☐ Weekly (No Security In-Depth) ☐ *VALIDATION:*	☐	☐	☐
8-502b	If restricted or IS protected area, is the IS downgraded before/after use? *VALIDATION:*	☐	☐	☐
	If seals are used to detect unauthorized modification, are the website guidelines followed? *VALIDATION:*	☐	☐	☐
	If seals are used, does the audit log reflect why the seal was replaced? *VALIDATION:*	☐	☐	☐
8-308c	Is visual access to the IS or classified information obtainable by unauthorized individuals? *VALIDATION:*	☐	☐	☐

T. INFORMATION SYSTEMS				
NISPOM REF:	**Question:**	**YES**	**NO**	**N/A**
	Software			
NISPOM REF:	Are contractor personnel that handle system or security related software appropriately cleared? *VALIDATION:*	☐	☐	☐
8-302a	Are the installation procedures identified in the SSP being followed? *VALIDATION:*	☐	☐	☐
8-306c	Is the media on which software resides write-protected and marked as unclassified? *VALIDATION:*	☐	☐	☐
8-306c	Is non-changeable media (e.g. CD read-only) appropriately handled and marked? *VALIDATION:*	☐	☐	☐
8-202c	Is security relevant software evaluated before use? *VALIDATION:*	☐	☐	☐
8-305	Is software from an unknown or suspect origin used? *VALIDATION:*	☐	☐	☐
8-305	If used, is the software from an unknown or suspect origin validated before use? *VALIDATION:*	☐	☐	☐

T. INFORMATION SYSTEMS

NISPOM REF:	Question:	YES	NO	N/A
8-305	Is software tested for malicious code and viruses before use? *VALIDATION:*	☐	☐	☐
8-305	Are incidents involving malicious software handled in accordance with SSP procedures? *VALIDATION:*	☐	☐	☐
8-502d	Is separate media maintained for periods processing? *VALIDATION:*	☐	☐	☐
	Media			
8-306	Is media marked to the classification level of the data? *VALIDATION:*	☐	☐	☐
5-300	Is media appropriately safeguarded when not in use? *VALIDATION:*	☐	☐	☐
	Are approved procedures followed when unclassified media is introduced into the system? *VALIDATION:*	☐	☐	☐
	Security Audits			
	Are all appropriate audit entries recorded? *VALIDATION:*	☐	☐	☐

T. INFORMATION SYSTEMS

NISPOM REF:	Question:	YES	NO	N/A
8-602a	Are processing times reasonable (i.e., hours between breaks)? *VALIDATION:*	☐	☐	☐
8-602	Are the protection requirements for each audit requirement recorded? *VALIDATION:*	☐	☐	☐
8-602a	Are the audit logs/records reviewed: Weekly? ☐ Daily? ☐ *VALIDATION:*	☐	☐	☐
8-602a	Is the reviewer authorized and briefed on what and how to review the audit records? *VALIDATION:*	☐	☐	☐
8-602	Does the reviewer understand his/her responsibility for handling audit discrepancies? *VALIDATION:*	☐	☐	☐
8-602	Are audit logs/records retained for 12 months? *VALIDATION:*	☐	☐	☐
Security Awareness				
8-103a	Has the contractor implemented an IS training program? *VALIDATION:*	☐	☐	☐
8-103a	Are users briefed before access is granted? *VALIDATION:*	☐	☐	☐
IS Operations				
8-502	If possible, have the user demonstrate the security level upgrading procedures. *VALIDATION:*	☐	☐	☐

T. INFORMATION SYSTEMS

NISPOM REF:	Question:	YES	NO	N/A
8-502	Is the user responsible for clearing memory and buffer storage? *VALIDATION:*	☐	☐	☐
8-502	If yes, does the user know how to clear memory and buffer storage? *VALIDATION:*	☐	☐	☐
8-502	Is magnetic media cleared/sanitized before and after classified processing? *VALIDATION:*	☐	☐	☐
8-310	Does the user understand his/her responsibility for handling/reviewing data and output (in-use controls)? *VALIDATION:*	☐	☐	☐
8-310	Does the user follow approved procedures when doing a trusted download? *VALIDATION:*	☐	☐	☐
8-310	If possible, have the user demonstrate the security level downgrading procedures. *VALIDATION:*	☐	☐	☐
	Maintenance and Repair			
8-304a	Is maintenance done at your facility with cleared personnel? *VALIDATION:*	☐	☐	☐
8-304a	If yes, is need-to-know enforced? *VALIDATION:*	☐	☐	☐
8-304b	Is maintenance done at your facility with uncleared personnel? *VALIDATION:*	☐	☐	☐

T. INFORMATION SYSTEMS				
NISPOM REF:	Question:	YES	NO	N/A
8-304b	If yes, are the maintenance personnel U.S. citizens? *VALIDATION:*	☐	☐	☐
8-304b	Does the escort understand his/her responsibilities? *VALIDATION:*	☐	☐	☐
	Does the audit log reflect the escort's name? *VALIDATION:*	☐	☐	☐
	Is diagnostic or maintenance done from a remote location using secured/non-secured communication lines? *VALIDATION:*	☐	☐	☐
	Is maintenance physically done away from your facility? *VALIDATION:*	☐	☐	☐
8-304b (4)	If uncleared maintenance personnel are being used, is a dedicated copy of the operating system software maintained? *VALIDATION:*	☐	☐	☐
8-304b	Is the system and diagnostic software protected? *VALIDATION:*	☐	☐	☐
8-304b	Is the entire IS or individual components sanitized before/after maintenance? *VALIDATION:*	☐	☐	☐
8-103	Has the ISSM approved the use of maintenance tools and diagnostic equipment? *VALIDATION:*	☐	☐	☐

T. INFORMATION SYSTEMS

NISPOM REF:	Question:	YES	NO	N/A
	Media Cleaning, Sanitization and Destruction			
8-502	Is the user responsible for clearing memory (volatile/nonvolatile)? *VALIDATION:*	☐	☐	☐
8-502	Is the user responsible for sanitizing memory (volatile/nonvolatile)? *VALIDATION:*	☐	☐	☐
	If yes, does the user annotate the audit records? *VALIDATION:*	☐	☐	☐
8-502	Ask the user to describe or demonstrate the procedure. *VALIDATION:*	☐	☐	☐
8-502	Is the user responsible for clearing magnetic storage media? *VALIDATION:*	☐	☐	☐
8-502	Is the user responsible for sanitizing magnetic storage media? *VALIDATION:*	☐	☐	☐
	If yes, does the user annotate the audit records? *VALIDATION:*	☐	☐	☐
8-502	Ask the user to describe or demonstrate the procedure. *VALIDATION:*	☐	☐	☐
	Is an approved overwrite utility used to clear magnetic media? *VALIDATION:*	☐	☐	☐
	If yes, does the user annotate the audit records? *VALIDATION:*	☐	☐	☐

T. INFORMATION SYSTEMS

NISPOM REF:	Question:	YES	NO	N/A
IA Website	Do you have approved procedures for the destruction of non-magnetic media (e.g. Optical Disks)? *VALIDATION:*	☐	☐	☐
	What level magnetic tape is used? Type I ☐ Type II ☐ Type III ☐ Unknown ☐ *VALIDATION:*			
	Does the contractor use an approved tape degausser to sanitize magnetic tapes? *VALIDATION:*	☐	☐	☐
	If yes, what level tape degausser? Type I ☐ Type II ☐ Type III ☐ Unknown ☐ *VALIDATION:*			
	If yes, does the user annotate the audit records? *VALIDATION:*	☐	☐	☐
	If yes, does the tape degausser comply with NSA specifications? *VALIDATION:*	☐	☐	☐
	Are approved procedures followed for clearing / sanitizing printers? *VALIDATION:*	☐	☐	☐
	STU-III/STE			
	If yes, are users briefed on proper use and security practices? *VALIDATION:*	☐	☐	☐

T. INFORMATION SYSTEMS

NISPOM REF:	Question:	YES	NO	N/A
	Are installed terminals supported by a COMSEC account or handcarry receipt? **VALIDATION:**	☐	☐	☐
	Are installed terminals in controlled areas? **VALIDATION:**	☐	☐	☐
	Does the SSP reflect the outside STU-III connections? **VALIDATION:**	☐	☐	☐
	If yes, has someone verified that the outside connections are authorized and accredited? **VALIDATION:**	☐	☐	☐
	Networks			
8-700	Are all outside network connections known, authorized, and accredited? **VALIDATION:**	☐	☐	☐
8-700e(3)	If the network leaves your facility, are NSA approved encryption device(s) used? **VALIDATION:**	☐	☐	☐
8-700b	Is this a unified network? **VALIDATION:**	☐	☐	☐
8-700c	Is this an interconnected network? **VALIDATION:**	☐	☐	☐
8-700c	If yes, does each participating system or network have an ISSO? **VALIDATION:**	☐	☐	☐

T. INFORMATION SYSTEMS

NISPOM REF:	Question:	YES	NO	N/A
8-700c	Does the network have a controlled interface? *VALIDATION:*	☐	☐	☐
8-610a	Is a network security plan being followed? *VALIDATION:*	☐	☐	☐
8-700	Is this a contractor only network? *VALIDATION:*	☐	☐	☐
8-700	If no, is a DISN circuit being used or has the customer obtained a waiver from DISA? *VALIDATION:*	☐	☐	☐
	If the network is not contractor only, has a MOU been coordinated between all DAAs? *VALIDATION:*	☐	☐	☐
	Are data transfers (receipt and dispatch) across the network audited? *VALIDATION:*	☐	☐	☐

U. COMSEC / CRYPTO

The primary source of information for COMSEC inspections is the NSA/CSS Policy Manual No. 3-16, August 2005. Requirements exceeding those in the NISPOM must be contractually mandated.

The NISPOM does not provide detailed guidance for protection of COMSEC material.

If you require training and audit information, contact NSA.

V. INTERNATIONAL OPERATIONS				
NISPOM REF:	**Question:**	**YES**	**NO**	**N/A**
	Disclosure of U.S. Information to Foreign Interests			
If YES, Continue!	Does your company have any classified contracts with foreign interests? *VALIDATION:*	☐	☐	☐
10-200 10-202	Was appropriate export authorization obtained prior to disclosure of classified information? *VALIDATION:*	☐	☐	☐

Remember that an export authorization is required before making a proposal to a foreign person that involves eventual disclosure of U.S. classified information. [10-202]

10-200	Is proper disclosure guidance provided by the Government Contracting Activity? *VALIDATION:*	☐	☐	☐
10-401d	Are requests for export authorizations of significant military equipment or classified material accompanied by Department of State Form DSP-83, "Non-Transfer and Use Certificate?" *VALIDATION:*	☐	☐	☐
10-202	Have the required security provisions and classification guidance been incorporated into the subcontract document for all direct commercial arrangements with foreign contractors involving classified information? *VALIDATION:*	☐	☐	☐

V. INTERNATIONAL OPERATIONS

NISPOM REF:	Question:	YES	NO	N/A
	Possession of Foreign Classified Information			
10-300	Has your DSS IS Rep been notified of all contracts, awarded by foreign governments, which involve access to classified information? *VALIDATION:*	☐	☐	☐
10-302a	Is foreign government information provided protection equivalent to that required by the originator? *VALIDATION:*	☐	☐	☐
10-304a	Are U.S. documents containing foreign government classified information marked as required by the NISPOM? *VALIDATION:*	☐	☐	☐
10-306	Is foreign government material stored in a manner that prevents its mingling with other material? *VALIDATION:*	☐	☐	☐

The receipt of classified material from a foreign source through non-government channels shall be promptly reported to the DSS IS Rep. [10-311]

10-312	Is the subcontracting of contracts involving access to foreign government information conducted in accordance with the NISPOM? *VALIDATION:*	☐	☐	☐

	International Transfers			
10-401	Do all international transfers of classified material take place through channels approved by both governments? *RESOURCE:* ISL 2006-01 International Transfers of Classified Material under Industrial Security Letters at: http://www.cdse.edu/toolkits/fsos/international.html *VALIDATION:*	☐	☐	☐

V. INTERNATIONAL OPERATIONS

NISPOM REF:	Question:	YES	NO	N/A
10-402	Is an appropriate transportation plan prepared for each contract involving international transfer of classified material as freight? *VALIDATION:*	☐	☐	☐
10-404	Does the use of freight forwarders for the transfer of classified material meet the requirements of the NISPOM? *VALIDATION:*	☐	☐	☐
10-405	Is classified material hand carried outside of the U.S.? If so, is such action always approved by the CSA? *VALIDATION:*	☐	☐	☐
10-405 b-c	Are couriers provided with a Courier Certificate and do they execute a Courier Declaration before departure? *VALIDATION:*	☐	☐	☐

Paragraphs 10-405a - j provide detailed requirements for employees acting as couriers when handcarrying classified across international boundaries.

10-406	Are all international transfers of classified controlled by a system of continuous receipts? *VALIDATION:*	☐	☐	☐
10-408	Is adequate preparation and documentation provided for international transfer of classified pursuant to an ITAR exemption? Note: For Foreign Military Sales (FMS) the GCA is responsible for the preparation and approval of the transportation plan. *VALIDATION:*	☐	☐	☐

V. INTERNATIONAL OPERATIONS		YES	NO	N/A
NISPOM REF:	**Question:**			
	**International Visits and Control of Foreign Nationals**			
10-500 10-508 10-509 2-306 2-307	Has a TCP been established to control access to all export controlled information? If yes, are these procedures current and effective? *VALIDATION:*	☐	☐	☐
10-501 10-506 10-507	Have you established procedures to monitor/control international visits by your employees and by foreign nationals? *RESOURCE:* ISL 2006-02 25. Q&A re Technology Control Plan (TCP)_Requirement When Foreign Nationals are Assigned to US Contractor Facilities under Industrial Security Letters at: http://www.cdse.edu/toolkits/fsos/international.html *VALIDATION:*	☐	☐	☐

Visit authorizations shall not be used to employ the services of foreign nationals to access export controlled materials; an export authorization is required in such situations. [10-501b]

10-506	Are requests for visits abroad submitted on a timely basis? *VALIDATION:*	☐	☐	☐

The Visit Request format is contained in NISPOM Appendix B.

10-508 10-509	Do you properly control access to classified by on-site foreign nationals? *VALIDATION:*	☐	☐	☐

All violations of administrative security procedures or export control regulations by foreigners shall be reported to the CSA. [10-510]

	**Contractor Operations Abroad**			
10-600	Do any of your employees have access to classified information outside of the United States? *VALIDATION:*	☐	☐	☐

V. INTERNATIONAL OPERATIONS

NISPOM REF:	Question:	YES	NO	N/A
10-603	Has all transmission of classified information to cleared employees overseas been conducted through U.S. Government channels? *VALIDATION:*	☐	☐	☐
10-604	Are employees assigned outside of the US properly briefed on the security requirements of their assignment? *VALIDATION:*	☐	☐	☐

The storage, custody, and control of classified information required by U.S. contractor employees assigned outside of the US are the responsibility of the U.S. Government. Contractors are NOT allowed to store classified information overseas – all storage MUST be under the auspices of the U.S. Government.

NATO Information Security Requirements				
10-706	Are briefings/debriefings of employees accessing NATO classified conducted in accordance with the NISPOM, and are the appropriate certificates and records on file? *VALIDATION:*	☐	☐	☐

Remember that a personnel clearance is not required for access to NATO RESTRICTED, although a facility clearance is. [NISPOM 10-702 & 704]

10-709	Are all classified documents properly marked? *VALIDATION:*	☐	☐	☐
10-710	Have you received adequate classification guidance? *VALIDATION:*	☐	☐	☐

V. INTERNATIONAL OPERATIONS

NISPOM REF:	Question:	YES	NO	N/A
10-712a	Are NATO classified documents kept separate from other classified documents? *VALIDATION:*	☐	☐	☐
10-712b	Have the combinations to containers holding NATO classified been changed annually as a minimum? *VALIDATION:*	☐	☐	☐
10-713	Has all NATO classified been properly received and transmitted? *VALIDATION:*	☐	☐	☐
10-717	Are the accountability records for NATO classified maintained as required? *VALIDATION:*	☐	☐	☐
10-721	Are visits of persons representing NATO properly handled and is the visit record maintained as required? *VALIDATION:*	☐	☐	☐

W. OPSEC				
NISPOM REF:	**Question:**	**YES**	**NO**	**N/A**
None	Are OPSEC requirements implemented in accordance with contractual documentation provided by the GCA? *VALIDATION:*	☐	☐	☐

X. SPECIAL ACCESS PROGRAMS (SAP)

Reference:	Question:	Yes	No	N/A
NISPOM, NISPOM Supplement; and DoD Overprint to the NISPOM Supplement	Is this a potential site for arms control inspections under START, OPEN SKIES, Chemical Weapons Convention (CWC) or International Atomic Energy Agency (IAEA)? If Yes: Is the DoD component sponsoring or acting as the executive agent for a SAP providing arms control implementation guidance and direction? Reference: 11-704 DoD Overprint to the NISPOM Supplement.	☐	☐	☐
	Is there any Special Access Program contract activity at your company? **Note:** The FSO should discuss this with the senior management official of the facility.	☐	☐	☐
	If Yes: Remember that such programs are subject to NISPOM, NISPOM Supplement, DoD Overprint to the NISPOM Supplement or the JAFAN 6/0 - Revision 1 <u>and</u> Program Security Guide requirements. A self-inspection of the SAP(s) is required annually IAW 1-206e of the DoD Overprint to the NISPOM Supplement or IAW 1-206 of the JAFAN6/0-Revision 1. The Security Inspection Checklist is found in Appendix J of the Overprint and Appendix F of the JAFAN 6/0 – Revision 1. *VALIDATION:*			
	If Yes: During the self-inspection, it is important for you to coordinate with the internal Contractor Program Security Officer (CPSO) to ensure that individual program security requirements are being followed. *VALIDATION:*			

The Program Specific Self-Inspection Process

Your company may be one of the many NISP contractors performing on numerous classified contracts requiring the administration of a complex security program. The self-inspection of your security program can be time consuming and possibly very challenging. A technique that can facilitate your self-inspection process to help you determine your facility's security posture focuses on one or more classified programs and assesses your compliance with the security requirements involved with those programs. This technique for evaluating your facility's security program describes the program specific self-inspection process.

Are there any benefits to using the program specific approach when conducting your self-inspection? The program specific self-inspection can help you gain a better understanding of what your company's responsibility is for a particular classified program in addition to providing your insight as to what each person contributes to the effort. The following is provided to explain the program specific self-inspection.

Your DSS IS Rep puts great emphasis on providing recommendations and suggestions to *improve* your security practices. However, this can only be accomplished when you have a good grasp of your operations and the manner in which classified information is handled. By taking a detailed look at one or more classified programs and interviewing key individuals to determine what they do and how they handle classified information, you will be able to evaluate how well your facility's *overall* security program is functioning. Many classified programs require a variety of tasks such as manufacturing, report writing, testing, researching, transmitting, etc. In a program specific inspection, you select one or more programs to be closely examined.

This program specific self-inspection process usually begins with the interview of the program manager (in some facilities this could even be the President) to learn what the program or contract is all about. Start by asking for a layman's overview of the program and question the level of classified access required, the procedures for classifying information, what, if any, problems have been experienced, and who in the facility is responsible for what on the program. Follow these leads to interview other employees including technical, clerical, and secretarial personnel. During these interviews, explore all security requirements connected with the employees' responsibilities in the program such as classified material controls, classified storage, markings, classification management, transmission, disposition, security education, and reproduction. Elements of a more administrative nature, relating to the facility's security program, such as the review of JPAS/JCAVS records and briefing statements, are ordinarily covered by reviewing your records within the Security Office.

The main rule is: if an element is applicable to your facility's classified involvement, cover the element in your self-inspection and, whenever possible, consider using the program specific techniques illustrated below.

You may find that exploring one classified program is not enough to give you a "feel" for how well your security program is functioning. One program may represent only a small part of the classified activity that takes place at your facility. If that's the case, you will want to examine several, if not all, of your classified programs in detail. It's important that you explore each inspection element thoroughly to ensure that your facility is in compliance with the NISPOM. Your underlying concern is that classified information and materials are properly protected and that your employees are knowledgeable of their security responsibilities.

A Program Specific Self-Inspection Scenario

The following scenario illustrates a self-inspection conducted on a specific program. For the purpose of this example, it is not an all-inclusive inspection.

Fenster Dinwiddie, FSO of Capabilities Limited (CL), has decided to focus his self-inspection on the SCUD Intercept Countermeasure (SIC) Project, one of three classified contracts awarded to CL. As we join Fenster, he has accomplished most of the administrative portion of the inspection. He has reviewed JPAS/JCAVS records, records of briefings, etc. and has completed his inventory of all classified materials and records. He has already touched base with the President of CL to make sure there were no recent organizational changes or foreign involvement that he should report. Certain elements like Subcontracting, Consulting, COMSEC, and International Operations do not apply.

Emulating the inspection techniques of his IS Rep, Fenster has decided to go out on the floor and find out what the employees do and how knowledgeable they are about their security responsibilities.

The Program Manager Interview

Fenster recalled that his IS Rep began each inspection by interviewing the person most knowledgeable about a particular contract. In this case it means talking to Conrad Floot, the lead engineer on the SIC Project.

Fenster went upstairs to "Engineering Row" to locate Conrad. "Fenster!" cheered the engineers as he entered the department. Fenster is always tickled to receive such a salutation. He feels honored to maintain such a congenial relationship with the engineers. After all, he does represent the security department.

"Say, Conrad, can you fill me in on this SIC Project of yours? I'm doing my recurring self-inspection and decided to focus in on your program." Conrad is impressed. No one has ever expressed that much interest in his project before and he loves to talk, especially about the SIC Project, his "baby" as he prefers to call it. "Sure, what do you need to know?"

"Well, why don't you start by giving me a program update? You know, what we're doing for the customer, what's classified about it, and things like that. But keep it simple, okay?" Conrad is thrilled. He proceeds to give Fenster a detailed overview of the program, its history, and current status. Fenster is thinking, "You know this is pretty interesting stuff. I should get out on the floor more often."

During the interview, Fenster took careful notes. He discovered that eight other engineers plus a contingent of secretarial and support personnel are working on at least some portion of the program. He decided he would interview each individual over the next couple of days. They discussed the classified design modifications which were being tested down the hall. Fenster had Conrad describe each step of the test procedure including whether aspects of the tests themselves were classified. He asked what makes the design modifications classified, how they're protected, who protects them, how and where they're tested, etc. To his relief, he found that all the procedures at least appeared to be in conformance with the NISPOM. Later, he would interview key members of the test and evaluation staff individually. He never realized there were so many security considerations!

Conrad identified his customer point-of-contact just in case Fenster or the IS Rep needed to call. They spent a lot of time on classification management. Fenster wanted to know what classification guidance had been provided by the customer and whether he felt that it was adequate. He asked what Conrad would do if they were to experience problems in determining what should be classified. They reviewed classified marking procedures, the kind of classified information that's been received, who is allowed access, procedures for generating classified information, reproduction, disposition, transmission, public release, and access authorizations. By the time he was done, Fenster had a pretty good idea of what the SIC Project was all about and whom to talk to for more information.

In addition to addressing the program-specific security concerns, Fenster remembered to question Conrad regarding important overall security program-related issues such as security education, adverse information, and foreign travel.

Employee Interviews

Next, Fenster interviewed each of the engineers on the project. He asked many of the same questions, but this time he was more interested in learning exactly what each person's responsibilities were and how they handled classified information. He already knew a great deal about the program just by talking to Conrad. It was time to "zero in" on the nuts and bolts of the SIC Project. His first stop was at Elmo Platz's office. According to Conrad, Elmo has been involved in the program from the start and, as the assistant program head, has major responsibilities.

First, Fenster asked Elmo to explain his job and how it relates to the SIC Project. Fenster asked what level of access he needed for the job, how he obtained his classification guidance, and whether there were any problems in this area that he should be aware of.

There were other questions as well, all designed to determine whether Elmo and his SIC Project staff were following the requirements of the NISPOM. Fenster asked:

☐ How often and under what circumstances did Elmo access classified information?

☐ Was he aware of his adverse information reporting responsibilities?

☐ Did he generate classified material in-house and, if so, on what equipment?

☐ How was the information protected?

☐ Did he know the combination to the security container? Was the combination properly safeguarded?

☐ Did he attend any classified meetings at the customer's site or at CL? Did anyone else from CL attend?

☐ Did he reproduce classified material? On what equipment?

☐ Was he familiar with the rules on retention, handcarrying, "need-to-know," marking, accountability, and disposition of classified information?

☐ Was he aware of any unreported security violations?

☐ Did any of his classified work require a special briefing, e.g., NATO?

☐ Was there anything relating to security that he thought Fenster should know about?

☐ Did he have any classified information that was not logged into the facility's accountability or Information Management System? Where did it come from?

You can see that Fenster was trying to cover all of the relevant inspection elements listed in the self-inspection handbook during his interview. This line of questioning was continued with each of the major participants in the SIC Program, from the engineering staff to the mailroom personnel. When appropriate, Fenster pretended to be from Missouri and asked the employees he interviewed to "show him" how they accomplished their various security tasks. When he was done, Fenster had covered every pertinent self-inspection element and had discovered only one or two administrative errors. His self-inspection was a success.

We hope yours is, too!

Center for Development of Security Excellence (CDSE)
Security Education, Training and Awareness Directorate
Defense Security Service 938 Elkridge Landing Road
Linthicum, MD 21090
www.cdse.edu